A Note From Rick Renner

I am on a personal quest to see a "revival of the Bible" so people can establish their lives on a firm foundation that will stand strong and endure the test when the end-time storm winds begin to intensify.

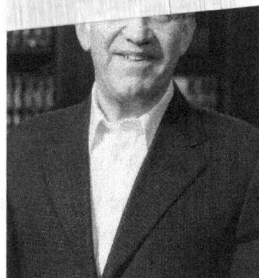

In order to experience a revival of the Bible in your personal life, it is important to take time each day to read, receive, and apply its truths to your life. James tells us that if we will continue in the perfect law of liberty — refusing to be forgetful hearers but determined to be doers — we will be blessed in our ways. As you watch or listen to the programs in this series and work through this corresponding study guide, I trust that you will search the Scriptures and allow the Holy Spirit to help you hear something new from God's Word that applies specifically to your life. I encourage you to be a doer of the Word that He reveals to you. Whatever the cost, I assure you — it will be worth it.

> Thy words were found, and I did eat them;
> and thy word was unto me the joy and rejoicing of mine heart:
> for I am called by thy name, O Lord God of hosts.
> — Jeremiah 15:16

Your brother and friend in Jesus Christ,

Rick Renner

Lauching Out Into New Territory

Copyright © 2020 by Rick Renner
8316 E. 73rd St.
Tulsa, Oklahoma 74133

Published by Rick Renner Ministries
www.renner.org

ISBN 13: 978-1-68031-612-4

eBook ISBN 13: 978-1-68031-650-6

How To Use This Study Guide

This five-lesson study guide corresponds to *"Launching Out Into New Territory" With Rick Renner* (Renner TV). Each lesson in this study guide covers a topic that is addressed during the program series, with questions and references supplied to draw you deeper into your own private study of the Scriptures on this subject.

To derive the most benefit from this study guide, consider the following:

First, watch or listen to the program prior to working through the corresponding lesson in this guide. (Programs can also be viewed at **renner.org** by clicking on the Media/Archives links.)

Second, take the time to look up the scriptures included in each lesson. Prayerfully consider their application to your own life.

Third, use a journal or notebook to make note of your answers to each lesson's Study Questions and Practical Application challenges.

Fourth, invest specific time in prayer and in the Word of God to consult with the Holy Spirit. Write down the scriptures or insights He reveals to you about being filled with the Spirit and empowered by Him in your daily life.

Finally, take action! Whatever the Lord tells you to do according to His Word, do it.

For added insights on this subject, it is recommended that you obtain Rick Renner's book *Chosen By God: God Has Chosen You for a Divine Assignment — Will You Dare To Fulfill It?* You may also select from Rick's other available resources by placing your order at **renner.org** or by calling 1-800-742-5593.

TOPIC

Paul Departs From Antioch

SCRIPTURES

1. **Acts 11:19-26** — Now they which were scattered abroad upon the persecution that arose about Stephen travelled as far as Phenice, and Cyprus, and Antioch, preaching the word to none but unto the Jews only. And some of them were men of Cyprus and Cyrene, which, when they were come to Antioch, spake unto the Grecians, preaching the Lord Jesus. And the hand of the Lord was with them: and a great number believed, and turned unto the Lord. Then tidings of these things came unto the ears of the church which was in Jerusalem: and they sent forth Barnabas, that he should go as far as Antioch. Who, when he came, and had seen the grace of God, was glad, and exhorted them all, that with purpose of heart they would cleave unto the Lord. For he was a good man, and full of the Holy Ghost and of faith: and much people was added unto the Lord. Then departed Barnabas to Tarsus, for to seek Saul: And when he had found him, he brought him unto Antioch....

2. **Acts 13:1-4** — Now there were in the church that was at Antioch certain prophets and teachers; as Barnabas, and Simeon that was called Niger, and Lucius of Cyrene, and Manaen, which had been brought up with Herod the tetrarch, and Saul. As they ministered to the Lord, and fasted, the Holy Ghost said, Separate me Barnabas and Saul for the work whereunto I have called them. And when they had fasted and prayed, and laid their hands on them, they sent them away. So they, being sent forth by the Holy Ghost, departed unto Seleucia; and from thence they sailed to Cyprus.

GREEK WORDS

1. "scattered abroad" — **διασπορά** (*diaspora*): the random scattering of seed; used to depict the scattering of Jewish believers
2. "persecution" — **θλῖψις** (*thlipsis*): great pressure; crushing pressure; to suffocate; a horribly tight, life-threatening squeeze

3. "a great number" — πολύς τε ἀριθμὸς (*polus te arithmos*): πολύς (*polus*) means "much"; τε (**te**) means "then; at that time"; ἀριθμὸς (*arithmos*) means "a fixed and known number" and is the root for the word "arithmetic"; together these words picture a massive amount of people who came together at one precise time; not a guessed number, but mathematically counted and known as a fixed number

4. "turned" — ἐπιστρέφω (*epistrepho*): to turn around; to physically turn; not a metaphorical change, but a real change that can be witnessed by outside observers; outward change that accompanies genuine repentance

5. "unto" — ἐπί (*epi*): upon; leaning fully upon; resting one's weight upon

6. "Lord" — κύριος (*kurios*): lord or supreme master

7. "seen" — ὁράω (*horao*): to see; behold; perceive; delightfully view; a scrutinizing look; to look with the intent to examine; to fully view; to experience; to know from personal observation

8. "exhorted" — παρακαλέω (*parakaleo*) begging; pleading; used militarily to encourage the troops

9. "purpose" — πρόθεσις (*prothesis*): to determine; to predetermine in advance; a decision set in stone from which one is never to deviate

10. "cleave" — προσμένω (*prosmeno*): to actively cleave; to adhere to; to remain attached to

11. "seek" — ἀναζητέω (*anadzeteo*): to earnestly seek; to search up and down; to make a thorough investigation; pictures a persistent and determined seeking

12. "brought" — ἄγω (*ago*): to lead: often depicted animals led by a rope tied around their necks; this word forms the root for the Greek word ἀγών (*agon*), which describes an intense conflict, such as a struggle in a wrestling match or a struggle of the human will

13. "ministered" — λειτουργέω (*leitourgeo*): pictures one who serves full-time as a priest; to perform spiritual service

14. "sent them away" — ἀπολύω (*apoluo*): to loose from; to release away; to set free; to divorce; a release from an existing bond, relationship, or responsibility

SYNOPSIS

The five lessons in this study on *Launching Out Into New Territory* will focus on the ministry life of the apostle Paul and include the topics:

- Paul Departs From Antioch
- Paul Departs From Corinth
- Paul Departs From Ephesus
- Paul Departs From Ephesus Again
- Paul Departs From Asia

The ancient port of Seleucia is located on the Mediterranean Sea in the area of southern Turkey, not too far from the Syrian border. Historically, it is important for a number of reasons — one being it was the location from which the apostle Paul first launched out to begin his apostolic ministry. We read about this in Acts 13:4.

It is important to note that Paul did not begin his ministry on his own initiative. The Bible says that he and Barnabas were selected and sent out by the Holy Spirit. As he embarked on his journey, he was totally unaware of what was ahead. He did not know about any of the challenges he would face or the amazing signs and wonders that the Holy Spirit would manifest at his hands. All he had was a word from God and the confirmation that it was time to launch out, and so he moved forward.

Think about it: When God called Noah to build the ark, He gave him very specific directions on what to do. Likewise, when He called Abraham, Moses, and Joshua, He gave each of them the clear instructions they needed to step out into the new territory to which He was calling them.

The same is true for you. When God calls you to step out and do something for Him, you will not know everything that is going to happen in your future. Nevertheless, He will give you what you need to know and His confirmation that it is time to step out and start what He has told you to do.

The emphasis of this lesson:

When God calls someone to do something, He gives very specific instructions. All you need in order to start and step out into what He has called you to do is His sure word of direction.

How the Apostle Paul Got Started

We know from Scripture that the apostle Paul — previously known as Saul — surrendered his life to the lordship of Jesus on the road to Damascus (*see* Acts 9:1-6). Shortly thereafter, he came to the city of Jerusalem to join himself to the disciples, "…but they were afraid of him, and believed not that he was a disciple (Acts 9:26). The truth is, while Paul's heart was totally renewed by the Spirit, his character was still very rough around the edges.

Yet despite his immaturity, Barnabas was drawn to Paul and took him under his wing. He brought Paul to the apostles and introduced him to them. Unfortunately, Paul did not understand submission to Church authority, and he ended up causing quite a disturbance in Jerusalem while he was there. When the apostles saw that the Grecians were about to kill Paul, they put him on a boat and sent him back to his hometown of Tarsus (*see* Acts 9:29, 30). The Bible says, "Then had the churches rest throughout all Judea and Galilee and Samaria, and were edified…" (Acts 9:31).

Time passed, and the Scripture says, "Now they which were scattered abroad upon the persecution that arose about Stephen travelled as far as Phenice, and Cyprus, and Antioch, preaching the word to none but unto the Jews only" (Acts 11:19). The words "scattered abroad" is the Greek word *diaspora*, and it describes *the random scattering of seed*. It was used to depict the scattering of Jewish believers, who were literally uprooted from their homes and communities and scattered like seed into new territory.

The *diaspora*, or scattering, was the result of "persecution," which is the Greek word *thlipsis*. This describes *great pressure* or *crushing pressure*. It can also mean *to suffocate* and signifies *a horribly tight, life-threatening squeeze*. The believers in Jerusalem were under this kind of pressure, and all of this occurred right around the time that Stephen was martyred (*see* Acts 7:54-60). Out of this tragedy, came the triumphant preaching of the Gospel that gave birth to new believers in all the lands where members of the Church had been dispersed.

The Church of Antioch

Church tradition states that the Church in Antioch was founded by Peter in about A.D. 34. Peter was called as an apostle to the Jews, and he focused on that call when he preached to the Jewish community in

Antioch. What is interesting is the shift that took place in this church, which is noted in Acts 11:20 and 21. It says, "And some of them were men of Cyprus and Cyrene, which, when they were come to Antioch, spake unto the Grecians, preaching the Lord Jesus. And the hand of the Lord was with them: and a great number believed, and turned unto the Lord."

Notice the phrase "a great number." In Greek, it is the words *polus te arithmos*. The word *polus* means *much*; the word *te* means *then* or *at that time*; and the word *arithmos* means *a fixed and known number* — it is the root for the word *arithmetic*. Together, these words picture *a massive amount of people who came together at one precise time*, and this massive number of individuals that got saved was mathematically counted and known as a fixed number. There was no guesswork involved.

The Bible says these people "…turned unto the Lord." In Greek, the word "turned" is *epistrepho*, and it means *to turn around* or *to physically turn*. It is not a metaphorical change; it is *a real change that can be witnessed by outside observers*. This word can also describe an outward change that accompanies genuine repentance. When a person truly repents, there is an undeniable change that can be seen by others.

When the people in Antioch "turned," they turned "unto the Lord." The word "unto" is the Greek word *epi*, which means *upon*; *leaning fully upon*; or *resting one's weight upon*. These individuals experienced a genuine saving faith as they placed their faith "upon" (*epi*) the "Lord." The word "Lord" is the Greek word *kurios*, which means *lord* or *supreme master*.

Barnabas 'Exhorted' the New Believers

Acts 11:22 goes on to say, "Then tidings of these things came unto the ears of the church which was in Jerusalem: and they sent forth Barnabas, that he should go as far as Antioch." What's interesting is that when Barnabas arrived in Antioch, Scripture says he "…had seen the grace of God…" (Acts 11:23). This tells us that when the grace of God is in operation, it can be seen — there is a visible demonstration.

The word "seen" is the Greek word *horao*, which means *to see*; *behold*; *perceive*; or *delightfully view*. It depicts *a scrutinizing look* or *a look with the intent to examine*. It can also be translated *to fully view*; *to experience*; or *to know from personal observation*. Thus, when Barnabas came to the Church of Antioch, he took a scrutinizing look at everything that was going on and noted it was a delightful scene of the grace of God being poured out among the people.

Barnabas was so excited about what he personally observed that he "exhorted" the people. The word "exhorted" is the Greek *parakaleo*, and it describes *begging* or *pleading*. It was used militarily to describe *the encouraging of the troops*. Basically, there was a new spiritual army emerging in Antioch, and Barnabas — one of the commanders in the Church — had been dispatched from Jerusalem with authority to plead with the new recruits to be faithful in their service to the Lord, regardless of the battles they would face.

Specifically, the Bible says Barnabas "…exhorted them all, that with purpose of heart they would cleave unto the Lord" (Acts 11:23). The word "purpose" is the Greek word *prothesis*, which is a compound of the word *pro*, meaning *in advance*, and the word *thesis*, meaning *to set*. When you compound the words to form *prothesis*, it means *to determine* or *predetermine in advance*; it signifies *a decision set in stone from which one is never to deviate*.

What did Barnabas plead with the new believers to do? He exhorted them to "cleave unto the Lord." The word "cleave" is the Greek word *prosmeno*, which means *to actively cleave; to adhere to*; or *to remain attached to*. These new Christians were actively cleaving to Jesus, and Barnabas was urging them to continue doing so for the rest of their lives. He wanted them to remain faithful to Christ and not deviate in their devotion.

Scripture tells us that Barnabas "…was a good man, and full of the Holy Ghost and of faith: and much people was added unto the Lord" (Acts 11:25).

Saul Was Sought Out by Barnabas

After the time of exhortation in Antioch, the Bible says, "Then departed Barnabas to Tarsus, for to seek Saul: And when he had found him, he brought him unto Antioch…" (Acts 11:25, 26). Remember, Saul had been sent back to Tarsus by the brethren in Jerusalem. The leadership there had felt as though he was not submitted to Church authority after creating such a ruckus in the city. Accordingly, they put Saul on a boat and sent him back to his home country. Since that time, he had lived alone with no connection to other Christians. Although he had been given a divine revelation of Christ, he had no relationship with Christ in the Church. More than likely, Saul was dealing with feelings of rejection and dissolution.

Barnabas went to "seek" Saul out. The word "seek" is the Greek word *anadzeteo*, and it means *to earnestly seek*; *to search up and down*; or *to make a thorough investigation*. It pictures *a persistent and determined seeking*. That is what Barnabas did when he arrived in Tarsus. He searched high and low throughout the entire city until he found Saul, and then he "...brought him unto Antioch...."

The word "brought" is a translation of the Greek word *ago*, which means *to lead*. Oftentimes, it depicted animals led by a rope tied around their necks. This word forms the root for the Greek word *agon*, which describes an intense conflict, such as a struggle in a wrestling match or a struggle of the human will. The use of this word informs us that when Barnabas found Saul, there was some sort of struggle to get him to go to Antioch. More than likely, Saul was still dealing with frustration over being deported back to Tarsus by the leaders in Jerusalem. In his mind, he had been burned by the Christian community and was resistant to rejoin them. In fact, he was so resistant that Barnabas apparently had to coax him to submit and journey with him to Antioch.

Maybe you know someone who was hurt in church and no longer attends. It may very well be that God has placed this lesson in front of you to prompt you to search for this "lost sheep" and help bring him or her back into the fold. What would have happened had Barnabas never gone out looking for Saul? We would not have the anointed, legendary writings of the apostle Paul.

Antioch: The Picture of the New Man in Christ

By the time we come to Acts 13:1, Saul and Barnabas were well established in the Church. Scripture says, "Now there were in the church that was at Antioch certain prophets and teachers; as Barnabas, and Simeon that was called Niger, and Lucius of Cyrene, and Manaen, which had been brought up with Herod the tetrarch, and Saul."

This was quite a mix of people. A cross-section of the leadership in Antioch reveals that there were two Jews, two African men, and one Roman. A cultural conglomerate of this kind was totally against society's standards and could only have taken place through salvation in Jesus

Christ. In Christ, skin color, ethnicity, and language differences all disappear. The Church of Antioch was a picture of the new man, and that is where Saul — soon to be the apostle Paul — was brought.

Acts 13:2 goes on to say, "As they ministered to the Lord, and fasted, the Holy Ghost said, Separate me Barnabas and Saul for the work whereunto I have called them." The Greek word for "ministered" here is *leitourgeo*, and it pictures *one who serves full-time as a priest*. Thus, the five leaders mentioned in verse 1 were all serving in full-time ministry.

Church history reveals that by this time, Saul had been a church leader in Antioch for about eight years. The church had become his home, and he was comfortable in his surroundings. Nevertheless, the Holy Spirit was now calling Saul and Barnabas to launch out into new territory. The Bible says, "And when they had fasted and prayed, and laid their hands on them, they sent them away" (Acts 13:3).

The phrase "sent them away" is the Greek word *apoluo*, which means *to loose from*; *to release away*; or *to set free*. It can also be translated *to divorce* as it describes *a release from an existing bond, relationship*, or *responsibility*. By using the word *apoluo*, it tells us that when the Holy Spirit said "Separate me Barnabas and Saul for the work whereunto I have called them," the two men didn't leave the next day. They had to go through a process of disentanglement, which took some time.

This lets you know that if God has called you to do something, you too will likely go through a process of disentanglement before you can launch out. There may be current relationships, responsibilities, or behavior from which you need to be detached or set free, and that is okay. When everything is said and done, you will be launched into new territory just like Saul and Barnabas were. "So they, being sent forth by the Holy Ghost, departed unto Seleucia; and from thence they sailed to Cyprus" (Acts 13:4).

STUDY QUESTIONS

Study to shew thyself approved unto God, a workman that needeth not to be ashamed, rightly dividing the word of truth.
— 2 Timothy 2:15

1. Paul's participation and years of service at the Church of Antioch were vital to his development and preparation for ministry. What does God's Word say about church attendance and the importance of fellowship in Hebrews 10:24, 25; Psalm 84:1-4, 10; Deuteronomy 12:5-7; and Proverbs 27:17?

2. When the grace of God is at work in a person's life, there is visible evidence. If someone were to take a close scrutinizing look at your life, what visible evidence of the grace of God might they see? What blessing concerning God's grace is promised in James 4:6 and Psalm 84:11? How are you to prepare yourself to receive God's grace? (Also consider 1 Peter 5:5.)

PRACTICAL APPLICATION

**But be ye doers of the word, and not hearers only,
deceiving your own selves.
—James 1:22**

1. As Saul and Barnabas prayed and fasted with fellow believers, the Holy Spirit spoke a clear word of direction to them concerning their calling. Has the Lord ever spoken specific instructions to you regarding a certain task or assignment? If so, what was it? If He hasn't spoken a clear word of direction, take time now to pray and ask Him what He desires you to do.

2. Once Saul and Barnabas had been called by the Holy Spirit and separated for His divine purpose, they underwent a process of disentanglement from which all that they were involved. Are there any responsibilities, commitments, or relationships from which you sense the Holy Spirit is asking you to disentangle? If yes, what are they?

3. Do you know someone who's been hurt in church and no longer attends? Maybe someone who is very spiritually gifted but believes they were mistreated and has since retreated from fellowship with everyone else? Who is God bringing to your remembrance that you need to seek out and help bring them back into right relationship with Him?

TOPIC

Paul Departs From Corinth

SCRIPTURES

1. **Acts 18:1,4-8** — After these things Paul departed from Athens, and came to Corinth; And he reasoned in the synagogue every sabbath, and persuaded the Jews and the Greeks. And when Silas and Timotheus were come from Macedonia, Paul was pressed in the spirit, and testified to the Jews that Jesus was Christ. And when they opposed themselves, and blasphemed, he shook his raiment, and said unto them, Your blood be upon your own heads; I am clean: from henceforth I will go unto the Gentiles. And he departed thence, and entered into a certain man's house, named Justus, one that worshipped God, whose house joined hard to the synagogue. And Crispus, the chief ruler of the synagogue, believed on the Lord with all his house; and many of the Corinthians hearing believed, and were baptized.

2. **Acts 18:11-16,18** — And he continued there a year and six months, teaching the word of God among them. And when Gallio was the deputy of Achaia, the Jews made insurrection with one accord against Paul, and brought him to the judgment seat, saying, This fellow persuadeth men to worship God contrary to the law. And when Paul was now about to open his mouth, Gallio said unto the Jews, If it were a matter of wrong or wicked lewdness, O ye Jews, reason would that I should bear with you: but if it be a question of words and names, and of your law, look ye to it; for I will be no judge of such matters. And he drave them from the judgment seat. And Paul after this tarried there yet a good while, and then took his leave of the brethren and sailed thence into Syria....

GREEK WORDS

1. "departed" — χωρίζω (*choridzo*): to separate; to part; to part company; to disconnect or to detach

2. "pressed" (in spirit) — συνέχω (*sunecho*): afflicted; pressured; forced; forced by outside pressure

3. "opposed" — ἀντιτάσσομαι (*antitassomai*): pictures an army that opposes another force; like a resisting army, the Jews assaulted and resisted Paul's liberating message

4. "blasphemed" — βλασφημέω (*blasphemeo*): to curse or to speak dirty or humiliating words

5. "henceforth" — ἀπὸ τοῦ νῦν (*apo tou nun*): from this moment forward

6. "I will go" — πορεύομαι (*poreuomai*): indicates traveling; a passage; a new direction

7. "Gentiles" — ἔθνος (*ethnos*): expresses the idea of different customs, cultures, and civilizations; people from every culture, custom, civilization, race, color, or ethnicity in the world; all the various races and colors of human flesh; all the cultures of the world; anyone not Jewish

8. "departed" — μεταβαίνω (*metabaino*): from μετά (*meta*) and βάσις (*basis*); the word μετά (*meta*) implies a change of direction; the word βάσις (*basis*) means "to step or to move the foot"; compounded, to move the feet in a new direction; to change the way one is walking

9. "joined hard" — συνομορέω (*sunomoreo*): next door; sharing the same wall with the synagogue; literally a few steps away

10. "chief ruler" — ἀρχισυνάγωγος (*archisunagogos*): the arch leader of the synagogue; the top leadership; the chief elder; one who gave oversight and management to the synagogues and who was responsible for everything connected to worship

11. "teaching" — διδάσκω (*didasko*): systematic learning of a student through the ever-present instruction of a teacher

12. "among" — ἐν (*en*): in or among; indicating he was continuously right in their midst

13. "insurrection" — κατεφίστημι (*katephistemi*): from κατά (*kata*) and ἐφίστημι (*ephistemi*); the word κατά (*kata*) implies domination or subjugation; the word ἐφίστημι (*ephistemi*) means to stand upon or to place over; compounded, to rise against with the intention to squash or to suppress

14. "one accord" — ὁμοθυμαδόν (*homothumadon*): an unplanned, spontaneous eruption at one precise moment; a unanimous outburst

15. "brought" ἄγω (*ago*): to lead: often depicted animals led by a rope tied around their necks; this word forms the root for the Greek word ἀγών (*agon*), which describes an intense conflict, such as a struggle in a wrestling match or a struggle of the human will

16. "judgment seat" **βῆμα** (*bema*): a platform on which a judge gave punishments or rewards
17. "drave" **ἀπελαύνω** (*apelauno*): to forcibly drive away; to push away
18. "took his leave" — **ἀποτάσσομαι** (*apotassomai*): from **ἀπό** (*apo*) and **τάσσω** (*tasso*); the word **ἀπό** (*apo*) means away and implies a severing and consequential distance; the word **τάσσω** (*tasso*) depicts order and something that is done orderly or intentionally; compounded, to intentionally and orderly withdraw or to remove oneself from a place; Paul was not haphazard or spontaneous in this departure, but it was a well-planned, organized, and thought-out departure, with nothing reckless or spur-of-the-moment about it

SYNOPSIS

As we saw in our previous lesson, the apostle Paul was brought from Tarsus to Antioch, where he joined a leadership team in the newly birthed church in the city. About eight years later, while they were praying and fasting, the Holy Spirit spoke and said, "…Separate me Barnabas and Saul for the work whereunto I have called them" (Acts 13:2). That day Barnabas and Paul received a specific word of direction from the Holy Spirit to launch out into ministry. Accordingly, "when they [the leaders] had fasted and prayed, and laid their hands on them, they sent them away" (Acts 13:3).

We saw in the last lesson that the phrase "sent them away" in Greek is the word *apoluo*, and although it sounds like an immediate departure, it is not. *Apoluo* is actually the word used for a *divorce*. When two people choose to divorce, they enter a transitional time of separation. Little by little, the two parties take the necessary steps to disentangle from one another in order to go their separate ways.

This is a picture of the word *apoluo*. It means *to loose from*; *to release away*; *to set free*; or *to divorce*. It is *a release from an existing bond, relationship*, or *responsibility*. When Saul and Barnabas were instructed to launch out, they couldn't immediately disconnect from their leadership roles and the people they had been connected with for so many years. They had to take some time to disentangle from their responsibilities in Antioch in order to launch out in the right way. By doing this, it lessened the likelihood of people being hurt or feeling abandoned.

In the several years that followed, Paul would travel extensively, ministering all throughout the Greek and Roman world. Eventually, he arrived
in the ancient city of Corinth where he met Aquila and Priscilla — a
marvelous couple that became a vital part of his ministry team. Together,
they would work to establish a thriving church in Corinth and then move
on to establish churches in other cities.

The emphasis of this lesson:

**The apostle Paul's time in Corinth was extremely fruitful. Once he had
finally submitted to God's calling and began focusing all his efforts on
reaching the Gentiles with the Gospel, divine favor, protection, and
provision came to him.**

Paul Experienced a Major Turning Point in Corinth

When we come to Acts 18, we find Paul in the midst of his second
missionary journey. Verse 1 says, "After these things Paul departed from
Athens, and came to Corinth." The word "departed" is the Greek word
choridzo, which means *to separate*; *to part*; *to part company*; or *to disconnect or
to detach*. The use of this word tells us that when Paul left Athens, he had
to part company and disconnect from what God was doing in the people
of that city.

In Athens, Paul had experienced a level of success in ministry he had
never experienced previously. For the first time, many Gentiles were open
and hungry for the things of God, and Paul had led several of them to
the Lord. But in order for him to move forward into the next phase of
ministry God had for him, he needed to disconnect from where he was
just as he had done previously in Antioch.

Of course, Paul began ministering in Corinth the moment he arrived.
Acts 18:4 says, "And he reasoned in the synagogue every sabbath, and
persuaded the Jews and the Greeks." Did you notice something different
about Paul's ministry in this verse? In Corinth, Paul's focus included
the Gentiles. He had just experienced success with ministering to them
in Athens, so his eyes were finally beginning to open to the ministry to
which God had called him. Again, God was giving him success in per-
suading the Greeks to Christ.

Then something happened. The Bible says, "And when Silas and Timotheus were come from Macedonia, Paul was pressed in the spirit, and

testified to the Jews that Jesus was Christ" (Acts 18:5). It is important to note the phrase "pressed in spirit" does not appear in most ancient Greek manuscripts. It simply says that Paul was "pressed." This word "pressed" is the Greek word *sunecho*, which means *afflicted*, *pressured*, or *forced*; it indicates being forced by outside pressure.

When Silas and Timothy — two of Paul's ministry companions — showed up, he felt compelled to redirect his ministry efforts back to the Jews. It is very possible that Silas and Timothy were shocked to see Paul ministering to Gentiles. All they had ever seen him repeatedly do was reach out to the Jews. Either directly or indirectly they put pressure on Paul to turn his focus back on the Jews. That is what the word "pressed" means.

As Paul attempted to share the Gospel with the Jews, once again, he was met with resistance. Acts 18:6 says, "…they opposed themselves, and blasphemed…." The word "opposed" is the Greek word *antitassomai*, and it pictures *an army that opposes another force*. Like a resisting army, the Jews assaulted and resisted Paul's liberating message of salvation through Christ, the prophesied Messiah.

Scripture also states they "blasphemed," which is from the Greek word *blasphemeo*, meaning *to curse* or *to speak dirty or humiliating words*. The Jews who Paul was speaking to in Corinth were so agitated by his efforts and activities that they began to rip him to pieces with their profane and humiliating words. Instantly, Paul shook off his raiment and said, "…Your blood be upon your own heads; I am clean: from henceforth I will go unto the Gentiles."

Basically, Paul told the Jews, "I am done with you, and my hands are clean." The word "clean" is the Greek word *katharas*, and it describes *a purging*. The use of this word was the equivalent of Paul saying, "I have worked you out of my system — I have purged myself of the desire to focus on helping you Jews."

Then he said, "…Henceforth, I will go unto the Gentiles." The word "henceforth" is the Greek word *apo tou nun*, which means *from this very moment forward*. The word *apo* describes *a separation*, which indicates that Paul was distancing himself from the Jews and his persistent efforts to bring them the Gospel. The phrase "I will go" in Greek indicates a declaration *to go in a new direction* — the direction of the Gentiles.

This brings us to the word "Gentiles," which is the Greek word *ethnos*, and it expresses *the idea of different customs, cultures, and civilizations*. It describes *people from every culture, custom, civilization, race, color, or ethnicity in the world; all the various races and colors of human flesh; all the cultures of the world; anyone not Jewish*. Deep in Paul's heart, he desired to see his fellow Hebrews saved, but he found little to no favor among them. In Athens and Corinth he began experiencing a level of success among the Gentiles that was amazing. Therefore, when the Jews in Corinth opposed and blasphemed him yet again, he made the Gentiles his primary focus. This was a major turning point in his ministry.

What Happened When Paul Shifted His Focus to the Gentiles?

The Bible says Paul, "...departed thence, and entered into a certain man's house, named Justus, one that worshipped God, whose house joined hard to the synagogue" (Acts 18:7). The word "departed" in this verse is significant. It is the Greek word *metabaino*, which is a compound of the *meta*, meaning *a change of direction*, and the word *basis*, meaning *to step* or *to move the foot*. When the two words are compounded to form the word *metabaino*, it means *to move the feet in a new direction* or *to change the way one is walking*. Essentially, Paul said, "I'm going to move my feet and get out of here! I'm taking my life in a new direction."

What's interesting about Paul's departure into a new direction is that he ended up in the home of a man named Justus "...whose house joined hard to the synagogue" (Acts 18:7). The phrase "joined hard" is the Greek word *sunmoreo*, which means *next door; sharing the same wall with the synagogue*. Paul had literally walked just a few steps away from where he had been. Although geographically he had not gone very far, mentally and emotionally the shift in his focus was miles apart. This was a huge step for Paul — a man who had been a Hebrew of Hebrews and former Pharisee from the tribe of Benjamin (*see* Philippians 3:5).

Paul's example lets us know that sometimes when you launch out into new territory, you don't have to go very far to begin doing something different. Physically, you may be in the same community or the same church, but mentally and emotionally your shift can be huge.

When Paul got into agreement with God and made the Gentiles his top priority, the miraculous began to take place. The Bible says, "And Crispus, the chief ruler of the synagogue, believed on the Lord with all his house; and many of the Corinthians hearing believed, and were baptized" (Acts 18:8). Crispus was the *arch leader* or *chief elder* of the synagogue — the one who managed and was responsible for all the synagogue's activities connected with worship. When he got saved, not only did his entire family get saved, but also many Corinthians, which specifically refers to non-Jewish pagans.

Acts 18:11 tells us that Paul "…continued there a year and six months, teaching the word of God among them." The word "teaching" is a form of the Greek word *didasko*, and it describes the systematic learning of a student through the ever-present instruction of a teacher. And the word "among" is the Greek word *en*, meaning *in* or *among*; indicating he was *continuously in the midst* of the Corinthians. For the first time in Paul's ministry, he had ample time to teach and pour the riches of God's Word into the people. Instead of being beaten, imprisoned, or kicked out of town, God gave him peace, protection, and favor with the people — for a year and a half!

God Delivered Paul From an Unexpected Insurrection

Eventually, opposition and resistance did arise, and not surprisingly it came from the Jews. The Bible says, "And when Gallio was the deputy of Achaia, the Jews made insurrection with one accord against Paul, and brought him to the judgment seat" (Acts 18:12). The word "insurrection" in Greek is the word *katephistemi*. It is from the word *kata*, which implies *domination* or *subjugation*, and the word *ephistemi*, which means *to stand upon* or *to place over*. When these words are compounded, the word *katephistemi* means *to rise against with the intention to squash or to suppress*.

The insurrection by the Jews was intended to squash Paul's flourishing ministry. The Bible says they rose up with "one accord" against him. In Greek, the words "one accord" describe *an unplanned, spontaneous eruption at one precise moment; a unanimous outburst*. Without warning, the Jews seized Paul and "…brought him to the judgement seat." The word "brought" is again the Greek word *ago*, which means *to lead*. It is the same word used to depict *animals led by a rope tied around their necks*. This word forms the root for the Greek word *agon*, which describes *an intense conflict, such as a struggle in a wrestling match or a struggle of the human will*.

Paul was brought against his will to the "judgement seat" of Gallio. In Greek, "judgment seat" is the word *bema*, and it describes *a platform on which a judge gave punishments or rewards*. After a year and a half of undisturbed ministry of the Word among the Gentiles, suddenly Paul found himself standing in front of the government official in Corinth being accused by a mob of angry Jews.

The Bible tells us they were saying, "This fellow persuadeth men to worship God contrary to the law. And when Paul was now about to open his mouth, Gallio said unto the Jews, If it were a matter of wrong or wicked lewdness, O ye Jews, reason would that I should bear with you: but if it be a question of words and names, and of your law, look ye to it; for I will be no judge of such matters. And he drave them from the judgment seat" (Acts 18:13-16).

The word "drave" is the Greek word *apelauno*, which means *to forcibly drive away* or *to push away*. The fact that Gallio "drave" them away tells us they did not want to accept his verdict. They actually stayed in front of the judgement seat begging and demanding for Paul to be prosecuted and punished, but Gallio would not do it.

Scripture says, "And Paul after this tarried there yet a good while, and then took his leave of the brethren and sailed thence into Syria…" (Acts 18:18). It is not clear exactly how long Paul stayed in Corinth after this incident, but it was an extended amount of time. Instead of being forced out abruptly, he "took his leave" when he was good and ready. The phrase "took his leave" is the Greek word *apotassomai*. It is from the word *apo*, which means *away* and implies *a severing and consequential distance*; and the word *tasso*, which depicts *order and something that is done orderly or intentionally*. When these words are compounded to form the word *apotassomai*, it means *to intentionally and orderly withdraw or to remove oneself from a place*. Paul was not haphazard or spontaneous in his departure; it was well-planned, organized, and thought-out, with nothing reckless or spur-of-the-moment about it.

The same way Paul carefully disconnected from the Church of Antioch, he carefully disengaged from the Church at Corinth. His time there and his task as the leading apostle, pastor, and teacher was complete. Once again, God was calling him into new territory. Therefore, he "…took his leave of the brethren and sailed thence into Syria, and with him Priscilla and Aquila… and he came to Ephesus…" (Acts 18:18, 19).

When Paul and his ministry companions arrived in the port of Ephesus, they disembarked and traveled down the Harbor Road into the heart of the city. Ephesus was a thriving, luxurious town saturated with pagan practices. Once again, a promising ministry opportunity was opened before them, and with it many unknowns — such as where they would live and how they would support themselves. But even with their unanswered questions, there was one thing of which they were sure: God had been waiting and was now ready to do miraculous things in their midst.

STUDY QUESTIONS

Study to shew thyself approved unto God, a workman that needeth not to be ashamed, rightly dividing the word of truth.
— 2 Timothy 2:15

1. When Saul and Barnabas were instructed to launch out, they couldn't immediately disconnect from their commitments and responsibilities. They needed time to disentangle properly and launch out in the right way. According to Isaiah 55:12, what are two primary characteristics of how God leads you out of one place and into another? Are you experiencing these mile markers as you move forward into what God is calling you? If not, pray and ask the Holy Spirit to show you what adjustments you need to make in your plan of departure.

2. It appears that when Silas and Timothy arrived in Corinth and saw Paul ministering to Gentiles, Paul was somewhat intimidated by their presence and changed what he was doing so that they thought good of him. What does Proverbs 29:25 say about the fear of man? (Also consider Matthew 10:28; Isaiah 8:12-14.)

3. Be honest: How important is what others think of you? Does anyone's opinion carry *equal* or *more* weight than what God thinks? If so, who is it?

PRACTICAL APPLICATION

But be ye doers of the word, and not hearers only, deceiving your own selves.
— James 1:22

1. Life is a moment-by-moment, day-by-day journey that is most often measured in *steps*. Oftentimes, God will only reveal to you one step at

a time, and before He shows you the next step, He will require you to do what He has already showed you. Be still for a moment and think: What was the last word of instruction the Lord gave you? Have you done it?

2. Again and again, Scripture reveals that Paul was called to be an apostle to the Gentiles (*see* Acts 26:17, 18; Romans 11:13). Yet for the first few years of ministry, he continued to focus on the Jews first, and he was consistently met with opposition. How about you? Have you reversed the priority of your calling? Are you doing what God has called and equipped you to do, or have you deviated from His plan? What kind of results have you been experiencing?

LESSON 3

TOPIC
Paul Departs From Ephesus

SCRIPTURES

1. **Acts 18:18-23** — And Paul after this tarried there yet a good while, and then took his leave of the brethren, and sailed thence into Syria, and with him Priscilla and Aquila…. And he came to Ephesus… [and] entered into the synagogue, and reasoned with the Jews. When they desired him to tarry longer time with them, he consented not; but bade them farewell, saying… I will return again unto you, if God will. And he sailed from Ephesus. And when he had landed at Caesarea, and gone up, and saluted the church, he went down to Antioch. And after he had spent some time there, he departed, and went over all the country of Galatia and Phrygia in order, strengthening all the disciples.

2. **Acts 19:1** — …Paul having passed through the upper coasts came to Ephesus….

GREEK WORDS

1. "took his leave" — **ἀποτάσσομαι** (*apotassomai*): from **ἀπό** (*apo*) and **τάσσω** (*tasso*); the word **ἀπό** (*apo*) means away and implies a severing and consequential distance; the word **τάσσω** (*tasso*) depicts order

and something that is done orderly or intentionally; compounded, to intentionally and orderly withdraw or to remove oneself from a place; Paul was not haphazard or spontaneous in this departure, but it was a well-planned, organized, and thought-out departure, with nothing reckless or spur-of-the-moment about it

2. "sailed" — ἐκπλέω (*ekpleo*): to depart by ship; to sail away

3. "enter into" — εἰσελθὼν εἰς (*eiselthon eis*): to enter directly into in a purposeful manner

4. "reasoned" — διαλέγομαι (*dialegomai*): to thoroughly discuss; to discuss every point of the matter; to discuss a subject from one side to the other; pictures a "going back and forth" in conversation to bring a listener to a fuller understanding of what is being discussed

5. "desired" — ἐρωτάω (*erotao*): ask, beg, beseech, or entreat; to earnestly ask; to passionately implore

6. "tarry" — μένω (*meno*): to stay, continue, remain, or abide

7. "consented" — ἐπινεύω (*epineuo*): approve or consent; he did not consent; in context, he was not in agreement

8. "farewell" — ἀποτάσσομαι (*apotassomai*): from ἀπό (*apo*) and τάσσω (*tasso*); the word ἀπό (*apo*) means away and implies a severing and consequential distance; the word τάσσω (*tasso*) depicts order and something that is done orderly or intentionally; compounded, to intentionally and orderly withdraw or to remove oneself from a place

9. "sailed" — ἀνάγω (*anago*): set to sea

10. "from" — ἀπὸ (*apo*): from; indicates a concrete moment in time when it occurred and the resulting distance that was felt

11. "landed" — κατέρχομαι (*katerchomai*): went down; to physically go south

12. "saluted" — ἀσπάζομαι (*aspadzomai*): to embrace by the wrapping of one's arms around; to salute; to wish well

13. "departed" — ἐξέρχομαι (*exerchomai*): leave, depart, or make an exit

14. "went over all…in order" — διερχόμενος καθεξῆς (*dierchomenos kathexes*): going through (the region) successively; again, it shows order in Paul's ministry; a strategy; a plan.

15. "strengthening" — στηρίζω (*steridzo*): fixed and solid, like a column that holds up the roof of a house; brace, shore up, bolster, support, or uphold; describes the act of adding strength and support to something already existing; used to describe a rod driven into the ground next to

a grapevine to support the grapevine as it grew upward; the supporting stake supported the clusters of grapes that eventually hung on the
vine; the grape vines were reinforced and supported by the rod

SYNOPSIS

In the first two lessons, we've seen how the apostle Paul got his start
serving as an elder with a handful of notable men at the Church of
Antioch. That season of ministry enabled him to work side-by-side with
both Jews and Gentiles for about eight years, which was a vital learning
experience he would need for his apostolic ministry to the Gentiles. From
Antioch, the Holy Spirit launched him and Barnabas into a traveling
ministry, taking the Gospel to multiple cities throughout the Greek and
Roman world.

After making stops in Cyprus, Asia Minor, and Macedonia, Paul made
his way down into Athens and where he experienced successful ministry
among the Gentiles. For the first time, he connected with many of the
pagan intellectuals and led a number of them to the Lord. From Athens,
Paul entered into the dark, pagan environment of Corinth where he met
and teamed up with Aquila and Priscilla and the power of God erupted
with many signs and wonders. Together with the Holy Spirit, they
established a powerful church there, and Paul taught the people for over
18 months.

When that time of ministry came to a close, Paul and Aquila and Priscilla
launched out from the port of Cenchreae and set sail for Syria. Eventually,
the trio made their way into the city of Ephesus, which was the fourth
largest city in the Roman Empire. Antioch was the third largest, having
about a half million people. It followed Alexandria, which was the second
largest city with a population of about a million. And Rome, of course, was
the biggest city in the empire, boasting of a population of approximately
1.5 million citizens.

Upon arrival, Paul began teaching in the local synagogue for about three
months. After experiencing another conflict with the local religious
leaders, he relocated just a few yards away to the lecture hall known as the
School of Tyrannus. There he began teaching the Word of God whenever
the facility was not in use. Amazingly, from that epicenter of education,
the message of the Gospel began to spread throughout the whole province

of Asia. Indeed, this was one of the most productive and effective seasons of Paul's ministry.

The emphasis of this lesson:

Like Paul, you, too, will experience different seasons in your life. The key is to know what season you are in and to focus on doing what God has called you to do in that time and place. Paul successfully did this in Corinth, Ephesus, Galatia, and Phrygia.

Paul Set Things in Order
Before Leaving Corinth

In our previous lesson, we saw how the Jews in Corinth suddenly created an insurrection against Paul and tried to squash him and his ministry. They brought him before Gallio, the head ruler in the city, and insisted that he be punished for his actions. But Gallio would not give into their demands. The Bible says, "And Paul after this [insurrection] tarried there yet a good while, and then took his leave of the brethren, and sailed thence into Syria, and with him Priscilla and Aquila…" (Acts 18:18).

Exactly how long Paul stayed in Corinth after the insurrection is not known. Nevertheless, eventually his time there came to a close, and the Scripture says he "took his leave." We saw that this phrase is a translation of the Greek word *apotassomai*, which is from the words *apo* and *tasso*. The word *apo* means *away* and implies *a severing and consequential distancing*; the word *tasso* depicts *order* and *something that is done orderly or intentionally*. When these words are compounded to form the word *apotassomai*, it means *to intentionally and orderly withdraw* or *to remove oneself from a place in an orderly fashion*.

Paul was not haphazard or spontaneous in his departure; it was a well-planned, organized, and thought-out departure, with nothing reckless or spur-of-the-moment about it. He knew God was calling him to the next phase of his ministry, so he prepared the church and put people in position so that ministry could continue once he was gone. He then told everyone goodbye and set sail for Syria.

It is important to note that everything that took place in Paul's life up until that moment had prepared him for the place he was about to land. His eight years in Antioch prepared him for his work in Athens, and his work in Athens prepared him for his extended stint in the city of Corinth. Likewise, his experiences in Corinth prepared him for his time in Ephesus. The same is true for you. Each previous phase of your life has prepared you for the present phase you are in, and all your experiences are working to prepare you for what lies ahead.

His First Visit to Ephesus Was Brief

Acts 18:19 says, "And he [Paul] came to Ephesus… [and] entered into the synagogue, and reasoned with the Jews." The words "entered into" in Greek mean *to enter directly into* or *enter in a purposeful manner*. Thus, when Paul landed in Ephesus, he immediately headed for the synagogue. This was the most logical place to begin connecting with people who had some biblical knowledge.

The Bible says Paul "reasoned with the Jews." The word "reasoned" is the Greek word *dialegomai*, which means *to thoroughly discuss; to discuss every point of the matter;* or *to discuss a subject from one side to the other*. It pictures a "going back and forth" in conversation to bring a listener to a fuller understanding of what is being discussed. This tells us that Paul spent quite a bit of time talking with the Jews in the local synagogue about the revelation of Jesus, building on their Old Testament knowledge.

How did these Jews respond? Scripture says, "When they desired him to tarry longer time with them, he consented not." The word "desired" here is the Greek word *erotao*, which means *to ask, beg, beseech,* or *entreat*. It can also be translated *to earnestly ask* or *to passionately implore*. Unlike many of the Jews Paul had reasoned with before, the Jews in Ephesus passionately pleaded and begged him to "tarry" with them longer. The word "tarry" is a translation of the Greek word *meno*, which means *to stay, continue, remain,* or *abide*.

Yet, regardless of the Jews' passionate pleas for Paul to stay, "…he consented not" (Acts 18:20). The Greek word for "consented" — *epineuo* — normally means *to approve or consent*. In the context here, however, it means *he did not consent; he was not in agreement*. He knew he needed to be moving on toward Jerusalem where God was calling him. Therefore, he "…bade them farewell, saying… I will return again unto you, if God will. And he sailed from Ephesus" (Acts 18:21).

What's interesting about the word "farewell" here is that it is the Greek word *apotassomai* — the same word used in verse 18 that is translated "took his leave." It is a compound of the word *apo*, which means *away* and implies *a severing and consequential distance*; and the word *tasso*, which depicts *order* and *something that is done orderly or intentionally*. When the two words are compounded to form the word *apotassomai*, it means *to intentionally and orderly withdraw or to remove oneself from a place*.

The use of this word lets us know that Paul did not abruptly or spontaneously abandon the people in Ephesus. When he said farewell to them, he calmly and carefully made his withdrawal, being mindful to preserve the relationships that were freshly formed. This is so important to remember to do when God calls you to do something new. He never wants people to feel abandoned as they are most important in His eyes. Paul was mindful of this and handled himself accordingly. We too must be mindful of people's lives and learn to disconnect from them gently as God repositions us.

From Ephesus, Paul Went to Caesarea

After setting out to sea, the Bible says Paul "...sailed from Ephesus" (Acts 18:21) and "...landed at Caesarea..." (Acts 18:22). The word "from" is the Greek word *apo*, which can be translated *from*, but it also indicates *a concrete moment in time when something occurred and the resulting distance that was felt*. The word "landed" is the Greek word *katerchomai*, which means *went down* or *to physically go south*. Thus, Paul could not and did not stay at Ephesus. In that moment, he made a decisive break and headed south to Caesarea.

In Israel, there were two cities with the name Caesarea. One was in the north in the region of Galilee, and it was called Caesarea, Philippi. The other was in the south on the Mediterranean coast, and it was called Caesarea, Maritime. This was a massive and magnificent port built by Herod the Great many years earlier. It was this southern location where Paul landed, and according to Acts 18:22, there was a church there.

Scripture says right after Paul landed, he went up to the believers "...and saluted the church..." (Acts 18:22). This word "saluted" is the Greek word *aspadzomai*, which means *to embrace by the wrapping of one's arms around*; *to salute*; or *to wish well*. When Paul saw the members of the Church of Caesarea, Maritime, he embraced them. This was a time of great celebration.

Acts 18:23 says, "And after he had spent some time there, he departed...." The word "departed" is again the Greek word *exerchomai*, which means *to leave, depart,* or *make an exit.* Once Paul was done visiting with the believers, he left and "…went over all the country of Galatia and Phrygia in order, strengthening all the disciples." When you read this in the Greek, it is a picture of Paul going throughout the region successively. Again, this shows order in Paul's ministry. Very few things did he do without a *strategy* or a *plan.*

In Galatia and Phrygia, Paul 'Strengthened' the Disciples

It is important to note that Paul's purpose on this particular leg of the journey was to *strengthen* all the disciples. The word "strengthening" in Acts 18:23 is the Greek word *steridzo*, which describes *something that is fixed and solid, like a column that holds up the roof of a house.* It means *to brace, shore up, bolster, support, or uphold.* It describes *the act of adding strength and support to something already existing.* This was the word used to describe *a rod driven into the ground next to a grapevine to support the grapevine as it grew upward; the supporting stake supported the clusters of grapes that eventually hung on the vine, and the grape vines were reinforced and supported by the rod.*

This is what the apostle Paul saw himself doing as he visited with believers in the country of Galatia and Phrygia. He pictured himself driving a stake in the ground right beside these believers, giving them the emotional, mental, and spiritual support they needed to mature in their faith and begin bearing abundant fruit. He did not stop along the way to plant new churches. His focus was strictly fixed on strengthening existing churches. This tells us that we need to know what our God-given task is in each phase of our journey and we need to stick to it.

Friend, never despise the place God has you. Where you have been has prepared you for where you are, and where you are is preparing you for where you will be in the future. And just as God raised up and prepared Aquila and Priscilla help Paul in ministry, He will raise up and prepare people to help you as well.

Eventually, Paul did return to Ephesus just as he told them he would. Acts 19:1 confirms this, saying "…Paul having passed through the upper coasts came to Ephesus…." Once he was back in Ephesus, he reignited his ministry — a ministry that would last for about three years without interruption. We will look at this period in detail in our next lesson.

STUDY QUESTIONS

Study to shew thyself approved unto God, a workman that needeth not to be ashamed, rightly dividing the word of truth.
— 2 Timothy 2:15

1. When you look back over your life, what are some of the seasons you can identify? What were some of the most rewarding events that took place in those seasons? Why are these events such a treasure to you?

2. Is God calling you into a new season? Has He been stirring up ideas in your heart that you can't seem to get away from? What do you sense He is asking you to do?

PRACTICAL APPLICATION

But be ye doers of the word, and not hearers only, deceiving your own selves.
— James 1:22

1. Before Paul launched out into fulltime apostolic ministry, he got his start serving as an elder for several years in the Church of Antioch. What are some of the early positions of ministry where God called you to serve? Name at least one lesson you learned in each of those positions that prepared you for the next season.

2. Are you experiencing a difficult time right now as you seek to do the will of God? Describe the conflict you are facing.

3. What was the last major conflict you experienced that God brought you through? What did He teach you in the process? How does remembering His faithfulness encourage you to keep pressing on?

TOPIC

Paul Departs From Ephesus Again

SCRIPTURES

1. **Acts 19:23-41** — And the same time there arose no small stir about that way. For a certain man named Demetrius, a silversmith, which made silver shrines for Diana, brought no small gain unto the craftsmen; whom he called together with the workmen of like occupation, and said, Sirs, ye know that by this craft we have our wealth. Moreover ye see and hear, that not alone at Ephesus, but almost throughout all Asia, this Paul hath persuaded and turned away much people, saying that they be no gods, which are made with hands: so that not only this our craft is in danger to be set at nought; but also that the temple of the great goddess Diana should be despised, and her magnificence should be destroyed, whom all Asia and the world worshippeth. And when they heard these sayings, they were full of wrath, and cried out, saying, Great is Diana of the Ephesians. And the whole city was filled with confusion: and having caught Gaius and Aristarchus, men of Macedonia, Paul's companions in travel, they rushed with one accord into the theatre. And when Paul would have entered in unto the people, the disciples suffered him not. And certain of the chief of Asia, which were his friends, sent unto him, desiring him that he would not adventure himself into the theatre. Some therefore cried one thing, and some another: for the assembly was confused; and the more part knew not wherefore they were come together. And they drew Alexander out of the multitude, the Jews putting him forward. And Alexander beckoned with the hand, and would have made his defence unto the people. But when they knew that he was a Jew, all with one voice about the space of two hours cried out, Great is Diana of the Ephesians. And when the townclerk had appeased the people, he said, Ye men of Ephesus, what man is there that knoweth not how that the city of the Ephesians is a worshipper of the great goddess Diana, and of the image which fell down from Jupiter? Seeing then that these things cannot be spoken against, ye ought to be quiet, and to do nothing rashly. For ye have brought hither these men, which

are neither robbers of churches, nor yet blasphemers of your goddess. Wherefore if Demetrius, and the craftsmen which are with him, have a matter against any man, the law is open, and there are deputies: let them implead one another. But if ye inquire any thing concerning other matters, it shall be determined in a lawful assembly. For we are in danger to be called in question for this day's uproar, there being no cause whereby we may give an account of this concourse. And when he had thus spoken, he dismissed the assembly.

2. **Acts 20:1,2** — And after the uproar was ceased, Paul called unto him the disciples, and embraced them, and departed for to go into Macedonia. And when he had gone over those parts, and had given them much exhortation, he came into Greece.

GREEK WORDS

1. "there arose" — γίνομαι (*ginomai*): something that arose unexpectantly; something not anticipated; something that took them off-guard

2. "stir" — τάραχος (*tarachos*): trouble; uproar; disturbance

3. "that way" — τῆς Ὁδοῦ (*tes Hodou*): the Way; the Road; the Path; enforces the singular belief that Christ is the only true way

4. "no small gain" — οὐκ ὀλίγην ἐργασίαν (*ouk oligen ergasian*): emphatically no small business

5. "craftsmen" — τεχνίτης (*technites*): in singular form, a craftsman or artisan; indicates a well-paid profession

6. "wealth" — εὐπορία (*euporia*): a compound of εὖ (*eu*) and πορεύομαι (*poreuomai*); the word εὖ (*eu*) means "good or swell"; πορεύομαι (*poreuomai*) depicts traveling; a passage; a transport; compounded, prosperous traveling; luxurious living

7. "persuaded" — πείθω (*peitho*): persuasion; one who is convinced, coaxed, or swayed from one opinion to another; convinced to the core; implies skill and time were needed to persuade him

8. "turned away" — μεθίστημι (*mesthistemi*): to change one's position

9. "craft" — μέρος (*meros*): part; role; share

10. "set at nought" — ἀπελεγμός (*apelegmos*): exposure; examination; rejection after examination; to be brought under examination; Christianity is a thinking faith

11. "temple" — **ἱερόν** (*hieron*): temple complex and the priesthood along with it; there were 6,000 priestesses in the Ephesian temple of Artemis

12. "despised" — **οὐθὲν λογισθῆναι** (*outhen logisthenai*): reckoned as inconsequential

13. "magnificence" — **μεγαλειότης** (*megaleiotes*): majesty; splendor; glory; magnificence

14. "destroyed" — **καθαιρέω** (*kathaireo*): pulled down; torn down; destroyed; dismantled; destroyed with nothing left standing

15. "world" — **οἰκουμένη** (*oikoumene*): inhabited world; the Greek-speaking world; Roman world and Greek civilization

16. "wrath" — **θυμός** (*thumos*): outburst of passion; uncontrolled rage, anger, or wrath; the word "full" is a translation of **πλήρεις** (*plereis*), which indicates fullness or "filled to the brim"; in context, full to the brim with rage, anger, or wrath

17. "cried out" — **κράζω** (*kradzo*): incessant screaming

18. "Great" — **Μεγάλη** (*Megale*): Great or Magnificent

19. "confusion" — **σύγχυσις** (*sugchusis*): confused emotions; a volatile mess

20. "companions in travel" — **συνέκδημος** (*sunekdemos*): fellow travelers; traveling associates

21. "rushed" — **ὁρμάω** (*hormao*): pictures a rapid motion; onrush; assault; spontaneous rush; emotional and uncontrolled impulse

22. "one accord" — **ὁμοθυμαδόν** (*homothumadon*): an unplanned, spontaneous and unanimous eruption at one precise moment

23. "would" — **βούλομαι** (*boulomai*): intending, resolving, determining, or planning

24. "chief of Asia" — **Ἀσιάρχης** (*Asiarches*): Asiarch, one of ten leading men in Asia connected with the worship of the emperor in the Roman province of Asia

25. "friends" — **φίλος** (*philos*): a relationship from which two or more have derived mutual value

26. "desiring" — **παρακαλέω** (*parakaleo*): begging; pleading; counseling; praying; even to provide legal counsel; a word used before troops went into battle

27. "confused" — **συγχέω** (*sugcheo*): jumbled minds and emotions; emotionally stirred up; commotion; upheaval; state of being out of control

28. "putting him forward" — προβάλλω (*proballo*): to thrust forward; to forcibly throw to the front

29. "townsclerk" — γραμματεύς (*grammateus*): city administrator; one of the highest officials in the city of Ephesus

30. "appeased" — καταστέλλω (*katastello*): to calm down; restrain; repress; to calm those who are aroused or incensed

31. "quiet" — καταστέλλω (*katastello*): to calm down; to be restrained; repressed; in this case, self-composed or self-restrained

32. "rashly" — προπετής (*propetes*): reckless; impulsive; rash; emotional intemperance

33. "robbers of churches" — ἱερόσυλος (*hierosulos*): robbers of temples; plunderers of temples; sacrilegious

34. "blasphemers" — βλασφημέω (*blasphemeo*): to speak crudely, rudely, disrespectfully, or discourteously

35. "cause" — αἴτιος (*aitios*): in context, no cause; no crime; no actionable offense

36. "uproar" — θόρυβος (*thorubos*): uproar; confused noise; disturbance; outcry; riot; turmoil; trouble that throws things into a state of disorder; emotions that spin out of control and that are accompanied by panic, hysteria, and emotional outbursts

37. "embraced" — ἀσπάζομαι (*aspadzomai*): to embrace by the wrapping of one's arms around; to salute; wish well

38. "departed" — ἐξέρχομαι (*exerchomai*): leave, depart, or make an exit

39. "to go" — πορεύομαι (*poreuomai*): depicts traveling; a passage, a transport

40. "into" — εἰς (*eis*): into; indicating direction and purpose

SYNOPSIS

Thus far, we have observed the life of the apostle Paul and watched how he first launched out into fulltime ministry from the Church of Antioch. We also saw how he spent over a year and a half establishing the Church of Corinth and teaching the people the Word of God. From there, he launched out in obedience and made his way to the city of Ephesus for a brief stay. He later set sail for Caesarea, Maritime and spent time encouraging the believers there before returning to his home base in Antioch.

On Paul's third missionary journey, he returned once more to Ephesus — this time making his way into the city by way of the interior roads, passing through the upper Gate of Magnesia. Immediately, he met 12 men who were disciples of John the Baptist. After leading them to Jesus and baptizing them in His Name, Paul laid his hands on the men, and they were all baptized in the Holy Spirit. He then spent the next three months teaching on the Kingdom of God in the local synagogue. But when the Jews' hearts were hardened and they began to speak evil of Paul, he moved his teaching ministry to the School of Tyrannus just a few yards away.

The renowned School of Tyrannus was located in the heart of the city, and every afternoon for two years Paul expounded the sacred Scriptures and explained how they connected with the Good News of Jesus Christ. The power of God began to explode, manifesting in miracles that Paul himself had never before seen. People came from all over Asia to hear him speak, and the mighty Church of Ephesus was born. Acts 19:18 says, "And many that believed came and confessed and showed their deeds." In the original Greek, this verse says *there was a stream of people coming*, and as the pagan population heard Paul proclaim the Gospel, they simultaneously believed and accepted Christ as their Lord and Savior.

Moreover, the Bible says, "Many of them also which used curious arts brought their books together, and burned them before all men...so mightily grew the word of God and prevailed" (Acts 19:19, 20). Amazingly, from the city of Ephesus, the Word of God went out to *all the people* who lived in the Roman province of Asia (*see* Acts 19:10), touching and transforming countless lives in extraordinary ways. Churches were established all over Asia — most likely, these included churches in Smyrna, Pergamum, Thyatira, Sardis, Philadelphia, Laodicea, Colossae, Hierapolis, and others. Paul was in the right place, and the right time, teaching the right people he was called to reach. For a space of about three years, he had a period of successful ministry in Ephesus with no recorded resistance. Then unexpectedly, something happened that would launch him out into new territory once again.

The emphasis of this lesson:

After three years of uninterrupted ministry, the craftsmen in Ephesus caused an insurrection against Paul and his associates. God used this unanticipated turn of events to launch Paul into new territory. Like-

wise, He can use unexpected obstacles in your life to launch *you* into a new place.

Acts 19 outlines the turn of events that forced Paul to leave Ephesus. Let's walk through the verses of this chapter, noting the key words and phrases that help reveal what actually took place. Beginning in verse 23, the Bible says:

> **"And the same time there arose no small stir about that way" (Acts 19:23).**

First, notice the words "there arose." This is a translation of the Greek word *ginomai*, which describes *something that arose unexpectantly; something not anticipated that takes you off guard or by surprise*. For three years, Paul had no resistance, and then something totally unexpected happened (*ginomai*). There arose no small "stir." The word "stir" is the Greek word *tarachos*, which describes *trouble, an uproar*, or *a disturbance*. In this case, the disturbance was about "that way."

The words "that way" in Greek actually read *the Way, the Road, the Path*. This was the Christian declaration that Jesus was not just *a* way — He was THE WAY. Although Christianity has been respectful of other religions, it has never been inclusive of them. Jesus is *the only way* to God, and that is what the people in Ephesus knew Paul was preaching.

> **"For a certain man named Demetrius, a silversmith, which made silver shrines for Diana, brought no small gain unto the craftsmen" (Acts 19:24).**

Diana is the Latin name for the Greek goddess Artemis, and she was the principal deity of the city. In Ephesus they did not use the name Diana; they used Artemis, but here it's translated Diana. In the city of Ephesus there was an enormous temple to Artemis, which was one of the seven wonders of the ancient world. In that temple there were 6,000 pagan priestesses that served, and people came from all over the world to worship in that temple.

Before leaving Ephesus, people would buy mini shrines as souvenirs to commemorate their pilgrimage to see the great Temple of Artemis. It was the silversmiths who made these trinkets — Demetrius being one of them. He was a "craftsman," which is the Greek word *technites*, meaning *a very well-paid professional* or *artisan*. Their business of making silver shrines was no "small gain," which emphatically means *not a small business*.

> **"Whom he called together with the workmen of like occupation, and said, Sirs, ye know that by this craft we have our wealth" (Acts 19:25).**

In this verse, we see Demetrius speaking to his trade union, declaring how they made their "wealth." The word "wealth" is the Greek word *euporia*, which is a compound of the word *eu*, meaning something that is *good* or *swell*, and the word *poria*, from the word *poreuomai*, which means *to travel*. When you compound these two words to form *euporia*, it describes *good traveling* or *luxurious living*. This tells us people in the First Century often equated their wealth with their ability to travel and to enjoy themselves. Demetrius reminded his fellow craftsmen that their wealth was due to their profession as silversmiths.

> **"Moreover ye see and hear, that not alone at Ephesus, but almost throughout all Asia, this Paul hath persuaded and turned away much people, saying that they be no gods, which are made with hands" (Acts 19:26).**

Here, Demetrius said Paul had "…persuaded and turned away much people…." "Persuaded" is a translation of the Greek word *peithó*, which means *persuasion*. It describes *one that is convinced, coaxed*, or *swayed from one opinion to another*. The use of this word implies that Paul used great skill over time to persuade and convince people to leave paganism and to come to Christ. In fact, Scripture says his coaxing had "turned away" many people. This phrase "turned away" is the Greek word *methistimi*, which means *to change one's position*. It can also be translated *to be perverted*. The apostle Paul knew these people were being converted, but in the eyes of the pagans, he was perverting people from their former faith to a faith in Christ.

> **"So that not only this our craft is in danger to be set at nought; but also that the temple of the great goddess Diana should be despised, and her magnificence should be destroyed, whom all Asia and the world worship" (Acts 19:27).**

First, the word "craft" here is the word *meros*, which indicates the artisans' *part* or *share* or *trade* in the business of making shrines. Demetrius said their "craft," which was all they had personally *invested* into the worship of

Artemis, was in danger of being "set at naught." The phrase "set at nought" is the Greek word *apelegmos*, which means *to be brought under examination and then rejected after examination*. The implication here is that Christianity is a religion that allows one to think. Thus, when Paul began to preach about the ridiculousness of worshiping Diana — an idol made with human hands and not a god at all — people in Ephesus began to think for themselves and examine the false religion for what it really was.

After their examination, many of the Ephesians rejected the worship of Diana. So much so that Demetrious claimed "…the temple of the great goddess Diana [or Artemis] should be despised.…" The word "temple" here is not the word *naos*, which we normally see. Instead, it is the Greek word *hieron*, which describes *a massive temple complex and all the priests or priestesses that worked within it*. In this case, there were 6,000 priestesses who served in the worship of Diana.

This brings us to the word "despised," which means *to be made non-consequential*. Demetrious claimed that Paul's persuasion was making the worship of Diana inconsequential and her "magnificence" was being "destroyed." The word "magnificence" is really the Greek word for *splendor, majesty*, or *glory*. And the word "destroyed" is the Greek word *kathareo*, which means *pulled down, torn down, destroyed*, or *dismantled*; *to destroy with nothing left standing*.

Essentially, Demetrious was saying, "If things keep going the way they're going, the religion of Diana is in jeopardy of being dismantled — even the temple itself could be pulled down. This could be both the end of our business and end of the religion of Diana whom all Asia and the world worshippeth." The word "world" referred to *all the inhabitants of the Greek-speaking Roman world and Greek civilization*.

On a historical note, Artemis was worshiped throughout the Roman and the Greek-speaking world and had two distinct forms. There was a western version, where her image appeared to be a huntress; and there was an Asian version, in which Diana looked like she was covered with multiple breasts. However, they were not breasts; they were bulls' testicles, which is a symbol of fertility. Clearly, the worship of Diana (or Artemis) was a very dark, devious religion.

"And when they heard these sayings, they were full of wrath, and cried out, saying, Great is Diana of the Ephesians" (Acts 19:28).

The word "wrath" here is the Greek word *thumos*, and it describes *an outburst of passion, uncontrolled rage, anger,* or *wrath*. The word "full" is a translation of the Greek word *plereis*, which indicates *fullness* or *filled to the brim*. Hence the phrase "full of wrath" means they were *filled to the brim with rage, anger and wrath*.

In response, the craftsmen "cried out." This is from the Greek word *kradzo*, which describes *incessant screaming*. Fueled by rage, these men began to *incessantly scream*, "Great is Diana of the Ephesians!"

The word "Great" in Greek is capitalized, and it means *Great* or *Magnificent*. And notice they didn't just say "Diana" — they said "*Diana of the Ephesians*." The reason for this stipulation was that their brand of worship for Artemis (Diana) was different from the rest of the Greek world. Theirs was more devious and dark. Although the rest of the Greek world imagined Artemis to be a huntress, in Ephesus she was known as Diana — the goddess of fertility covered with bulls' testicles.

> **"And the whole city was filled with confusion: and having caught Gaius and Aristarchus, men of Macedonia, Paul's companions in travel, they rushed with one accord into the theatre" (Acts 19:29).**

The word "confusion" describes *a volatile mess*. In the midst of a massive emotional breakdown, the inhabitants of the whole city seized Gaius and Aristarchus — Paul's *fellow travelers* or *traveling associates* — and they "rushed with one accord into the theatre."

The word "rushed" is the Greek word *hormao*, which describes *a rapid motion*; *an onrush*; *an assault*; *a spontaneous rush*; or *an emotional, uncontrolled impulse*. The words "one accord" in Greek describe *an unplanned, spontaneous and unanimous eruption at one precise moment*. Thus, in the midst of the volatile mess, the people suddenly snapped and erupted in a united, uncontrollable uproar.

> **"And when Paul would have entered in unto the people, the disciples suffered him not" (Acts 19:30).**

When the Bible says Paul "would have entered," the word "would" is the Greek word *boulomai*, which means Paul had *fully intended, resolved, and determined* to rush into the theater to help his companions. However, the Bible says, "the disciples suffered him not." "Suffered him not" in Greek is the equivalent of the disciples saying, "This is a bad decision, and we're not going to let you do it." Paul was about to make a major mistake, because he was acting in emotions, but his disciples stopped him. Thank God for friends who stop us when we're about to do something wrong.

> **"And certain of the chief of Asia, which were his friends, sent unto him, desiring him that he would not adventure himself into the theatre" (Acts 19:31).**

The phrase "chief of Asia" is the Greek word *Asiarches*, which was specifically used to describe *a group of ten leading men in Asia who were the representatives of the worship of the Emperor in the Roman province of Asia.* What's interesting is that these high-ranking, powerful pagan leaders were Paul's "friends" — the Greek word *philos*, describing *a relationship from which two or more have derived mutual value.* This tells us Paul was even able to be friendly with people with whom he did not agree. He was living in such a way that even these pagans felt camaraderie with him. Clearly, Paul was intelligent and demonstrated great power as he operated in ministry, and they respected him. This tells us that when we live right, we are able to win the respect and friendship of people that are not believers.

As strange as it may seem, these high-ranking pagan leaders were "desiring" Paul not to enter the theatre." The word "desiring" is the Greek word *parakaleó*, which describes *begging, pleading, praying, and counseling.* It was also a military term used to describe how commanding officers would encourage their troops before they went into battle. Using this word was the equivalent of saying, "If you do this, Paul, you're heading into a battle you cannot handle. We are legally counseling you and begging you not to take this action." Amazingly, both Paul's disciples and his pagan friends were prohibiting him from making a bad mistake.

> **"Some therefore cried one thing, and some another: for the assembly was confused; and the more part knew not wherefore they were come together. And they drew Alexander out of the multitude, the Jews putting him forward. And Alexander beckoned with the hand, and would have made his defence unto the people. But when they knew that he was a Jew, all with one voice about the space of two hours cried out, Great is Diana of the Ephesians." (Acts 19:32-34).**

In verse 32, the word "confused" is the Greek word *sugcheo*, which indicates *jumbled minds and emotions.* It depicts *a group of people emotionally stirred up* or *in an upheaval, a state of being out of control.* The people assembled were so confused, the Bible says, "…the more part knew not wherefore they came together" (Acts 19:32). This means the people didn't even know why they were there or why they were upset. At that point, everyone was just upset and caught up in an emotional frenzy.

A man named Alexander was in the crowd. He too was one of Paul's associates. In hopes that he could calm the people, the Bible says they "put him forward." In the Greek, "putting him forward" is the word *proballo*, which means *to thrust forward* or *to forcibly throw to the front.* Alexander was pushed forward in front of the confused and crazed crowd and began to motion with his hand for the people to settle down. But they would not. Instead, they ramped up their rampage and "cried out" for two solid hours, "Great is Diana of the Ephesians."

> **"And when the townclerk had appeased the people, he said, Ye men of Ephesus, what man is there that knoweth not how that the city of the Ephesians is a worshipper of the great goddess Diana, and of the image which fell down from Jupiter? Seeing then that these things cannot be spoken against, ye ought to be quiet, and to do nothing rashly" (Acts 19:35, 36).**

The word "townclerk" here is the Greek word *grammateus*, and it describes *a city administrator, one of the highest officials in the city of Ephesus.* The Bible says this town clerk "appeased the people." The word "appeased" is the Greek word *katastello*, which means *to calm down, restrain,* or *repress.* When he was able *to calm those who were aroused or incensed*, he spoke to them and attempted to assure them that their city's devotion to the goddess Diana was secure and not at risk. He then urged them "…to be quiet, and to do nothing rashly." The word "quiet" is again the Greek word *katastello*, meaning *to calm down; to be restrained.* In this case, he called them to be *self-composed* or *self-restrained* and not do anything "rashly," which means *reckless* or *impulsive.*

> **"For ye have brought hither these men, which are neither robbers of churches, nor yet blasphemers of your goddess" (Acts 19:37).**

In this verse, the city administrator clarified the character of Gaius and Aristarchus whom they had arrested. He said they were not "robbers of churches," which in Greek means they were *not destroyers or plunderers of temples or public facilities.* He also said they were not "blasphemers," which is the Greek word *blasphemeo*. This means these men were *not speaking crudely, rudely,* or *disrespectfully* of the religion of Diana.

The town clerk went on to say, "Wherefore if Demetrius, and the craftsmen which are with him, have a matter against any man, the law is open, and there are deputies: let them implead one another. But if ye inquire any thing concerning other matters, it shall be determined in a lawful assembly. For we are in danger to be called in question for this day's uproar, there being no cause whereby we may give an account of this concourse" (Acts 19:38-40).

In the Roman world, these kinds of outburst were not permitted, and if the Ephesians didn't calm down and grab hold of their emotions, they were in great danger of the Roman military invading. For a second time, the town administrator reminded the people that their riotous behavior had "no cause." The word "cause" in Greek is the word *aitios*, which in context here means *no cause, no crime,* or *no actionable offense*. Paul and his comrades had committed no crime or actionable offense that justified the revolt that had been taking place.

> **"And when he had thus spoken, he dismissed the assembly. And after the uproar was ceased, Paul called unto him the disciples, and embraced them, and departed for to go into Macedonia. And when he had gone over those parts, and had given them much exhortation, he came into Greece" (Acts 19:41; 20:1,2).**

The word "uproar" in Greek is the word *thorubos*, which describes *an uproar, confused noise, disturbance, outcry, riot, turmoil,* or *trouble that throws things into a state of disorder*. It is a picture of *emotions that spin out of control and that are accompanied by panic, hysteria, and emotional outbursts*. Once the uproar ceased, Paul called his disciples to him and "embraced" them. The word "embraced" is the Greek word *aspadzomai*, which means *to embrace by the wrapping of one's arms around; to salute* or *to wish well*.

Paul then "departed," which is the Greek word *exerchomai*, meaning *to leave, depart,* or *make an exit*. This departing enabled him "to go into Macedonia." The words "to go" are the Greek word *poreuomai*, which depicts *traveling, a passage,* or *a transport*; and the word "into" in Greek is *eis*, which means *into* and carries the idea of *direction* and *purpose*.

To be clear, this insurrection by the silversmiths in Ephesus was totally unexpected by Paul — it was a *ginomai* moment. Nevertheless, God used it to launch him into new territory. You too will face times when unexpected obstacles arise in your life, including challenges with people. Instead of being filled with sorrow, casting blame, or grieving over something you can do nothing about, ask the Holy Spirit for His grace to embrace the new place He desires to take you.

Friend, God has a divine assignment just for you. It is right in front of you in your future and it is calling your name. You are the only one who can fulfill it. You just need to know how to disconnect from where you are and embrace the new place He has called you to be. When you get into the right place and begin doing what you know in your heart God is calling you to do, your most miraculous days will begin to unfold right before your very eyes.

STUDY QUESTIONS

Study to shew thyself approved unto God, a workman that needeth not to be ashamed, rightly dividing the word of truth.
— 2 Timothy 2:15

1. After reading through this lesson, what is your initial reaction to all that you heard? What is your greatest takeaway that you can use in your own life?
   Paul could have pushed aside the warnings and urgent counsel of his friends and went into the theatre anyway, but he didn't. Instead, he chose listened to and received their counsel. How do these verses from God's Word illustrate that Paul made the right decision? (Also consider Proverbs 14:15-18; 15:5.)
   - Proverbs 22:3 and 27:12
   - Proverbs 11:14; 15:22 and 24:6

2. Second Corinthians 5:19 and 20(*NIV*) says, "God was reconciling the world to himself in Christ, not counting men's sins against them. And he has committed to us the message of reconciliation. We are therefore Christ's ambassadors, as though God were making his appeal through us…." How *appealing* would you say your life is to non-believers? That is, how attractive, interesting, and alluring are you to the non-Christians around you?

3. Paul's life demonstrated Jesus' words in Matthew 5:16 and the principle of Proverbs 16:7. Pray and ask the Holy Spirit to show you *if* and *where* your life demonstrates these truths.

PRACTICAL APPLICATION

But be ye doers of the word, and not hearers only,
deceiving your own selves.
—James 1:22

1. Paul was about to make a very bad decision, because he was acting out of emotions. But his disciples and heathen friends stopped him. Who in your life are you thankful for stopping you when you were about to do something dangerously foolish? What trouble did they enable you to avoid?

2. The Bible says Paul was able to have a level of friendship with members of the "chief of Asia," who were pagans with whom he did not agree. What unbelievers do you know that feel a sense of camaraderie with you — even though you have differing values and perspectives? Are you living your life in such a way that even unsaved people respect and honor you?

3. Many times the Holy Spirit will lead us by His still small voice within our spirit. Other times He will speak to us through fellow believers and even unbelievers as He did in this case with Paul. Has the Holy Spirit been trying to tell you something that you have knowingly or unknowingly ignored? Who has He placed in your path to echo this same message of warning and direction? What has He been trying to get you to hear and obey? What course adjustments do you need to make at this time?

TOPIC

Paul Departs From Asia

SCRIPTURES

1. **Acts 20:36-38** — And when he had thus spoken, he kneeled down, and prayed with them all. And [it happened] they all wept sore, and fell on Paul's neck, and kissed him. Sorrowing most of all for the words which he spake, that they should see his face no more. And they accompanied him unto the ship.

2. **Acts 21:1** — And it came to pass, that after we were gotten from them, and had launched, [having drawn away from them]....

GREEK WORDS

1. "kneeled" — θεὶς τὰ γόνατα (*theis ta gonata*): to bow the knees; to put the knees in position

2. "prayed" — προσεύχομαι (*proseuchomai*): from πρός (*pros*) and εὔχομαι (*euchomai*); the word πρός (*pros*) means "toward"; the word εὔχομαι (*euchomai*) means "a vow"; compounded, to draw near to make a vow in exchange for answered prayer; a sacrifice offered in exchange for an answer; the most common word for prayer in the New Testament; a prayerful business transaction

3. "with" — σὺν (*sun*): with; jointly; accompanied with; in partnership with

4. "it happened" — γίνομαι (*ginomai*): something that arose unexpectantly; something not anticipated; something that took them off-guard

5. "wept sore" — κλαυθμός (*klauthmos*): bitter weeping; emotional weeping

6. "fell" — ἐπιπίπτω (*epipipto*): to collapse upon

7. "kissed" — καταφιλέω (*kataphileo*): literally, to kiss down; to kiss fervently; to profusely kiss; to cover with kisses

8. "sorrowing" — ὀδυνάω (*odunao*): from ὀδύνη (*odune*), depicts intense emotional pain; anguish; a great personal anguish expressed by great mourning

9. "see" — θεωρέω (*theoreo*): to gaze at; to look upon; to discern; the root for the word "theater"

10. "face" — πρόσωπον (*prosopon*): face; countenance; to see one's eyes

11. "accompanied" — προπέμπω (*propempo*): accompany; conduct; escort; to help one on his way

12. "launched" — ἀνάγω (*anago*): set to sea

13. "having drawn away from them" — ἀποσπάω (*apospao*): from ἀπό (*apo*) and σπάω (*spao*); the word ἀπό (*apo*) means "away"; the word σπάω (*spao*) means "to pull"; compounded, pulling away from; withdrawing from; wrenching away from; tearing away from; indicates a difficult emotional departure

SYNOPSIS

The ancient city of Miletus played a very significant role in the ministry of the apostle Paul. As we learned in our last lesson, Paul had returned to Ephesus and experienced three years of uninterrupted ministry, especially among the Gentiles. Then suddenly and unexpectedly, a huge insurrection took place. The craftsmen of Ephesus that made the miniature shrines of the Temple of Diana were up in arms because Paul's ministry was severely cutting into their profits. He and his associates had become so effective at presenting the Gospel and showing people the truth about the worship of Diana that huge numbers of people from all across Asia were converting to Christ. Consequently, less and less were buying the trinkets made by the artisans.

Led by a firestorm of words from the mouth of Demetrius, one of the leading silversmiths in the region, the silver workers union in Ephesus became violently enraged and grabbed two of Paul's associates and dragged them into the city's theater, which seated about 24,000 people. On that particular day, about 20,000 craftsmen had packed the theater to listen to what Demetrius had to say. Upon hearing that their business was down and in danger of being crushed altogether, the mob became emotionally unhinged and volatile.

When Paul found out that his traveling companions were in great danger inside the theater, he determined to go inside to stand with and assist them. But his disciples pleaded with him not to go in. Surprisingly, even many of the top ten pagan priests who ruled all of Asia and oversaw the worship of the emperor begged Paul to refrain from entering the theater.

The Bibles says, "And certain of the chief of Asia, which were his friends, sent unto him, desiring him that he would not adventure himself into the theatre" (Acts 19:31). We saw that the word "desiring" is the Greek word *parakaleo*, which describes *begging, pleading, praying, and counseling*. It was also a military term used to describe how commanding officers would encourage their troops before going into battle. By using this word, it was the same as Paul's friends saying, "If you do this, you're heading into a battle you cannot handle. We're legally counseling you and begging you not to take this action."

Thankfully, Paul listened and did what his disciples and pagan friends instructed. He didn't enter the theater. Instead, he launched out from Ephesus and later came to Miletus, which was about 40 miles south of the city. "And from Miletus he sent to Ephesus, and called the elders of the church" (Acts 20:17). Without hesitation, the Ephesian leaders made the trip, and there they saw and heard from Paul one last time.

The emphasis of this lesson:

In spite of the riotous uproar created by the craftsmen in Ephesus, Paul found a way to connect with the church leaders of Ephesus one last time and complete his ministry to them. When the going gets tough, the Holy Spirit will show you creative ways to finish the assignment He has given you.

Paul Positioned Himself on His Knees in Prayer

As Paul shared his final words with the elders of Ephesus, he told them, "…Behold, I know that ye all, among whom I have gone preaching the kingdom of God, shall see my face no more" (Acts 20:25). Realizing this was the end of his ministry to these leaders he had poured into for three years, Paul wanted to make the most of the final moments they had together.

After sharing a prophetic glimpse of what would take place after he was gone and entrusting them to the word of God (*see* Acts 20:32), the Bible says, "…he kneeled down, and prayed with them all" (Acts 20:36). The word "kneeled" in Greek is *theis ta gonata*, which means *to bow the knees* or *to put the knees in position.* In New Testament times, getting on one's knees was synonymous with prayer. In Paul's final moments with the leaders of the Church of Ephesus, he put his knees into position and "prayed."

The word "prayed" in Greek is *proseuchomai,* which is from the words *pros* and *euchomai.* The word *pros* means *toward;* and the word *euchomai* describes *a vow.* When these words are compounded to form the new word *proseuchomai,* it means *to draw near to make a vow in exchange for answered prayers.* This word carries the idea of *a sacrifice offered in exchange for an answer.* It is because of the sacrifice of Jesus Christ on the altar of the Cross that we can draw near to God in prayer.

The most common word used throughout the New Testament for prayer is *proseuchomai.* Essentially, it describes *a prayerful business transaction.* When people prayed to God, they surrendered themselves to Him, and in exchange they expected Him to answer their request and provide for what they needed.

The Scripture says Paul. "...kneeled down, and prayed with them all" (Acts 20:36). The word "with" here is the Greek word *sun,* which means *jointly; accompanied with;* or *in partnership with.* This tells us as Paul and the elders from Ephesus positioned themselves on their knees, they began surrendering themselves to God and making vows or promises to Him, expecting Him to answer.

Their Time Together Was Deeply Emotional

Acts 20:37 goes on to say, "And they all wept sore, and fell on Paul's neck, and kissed him." What is interesting about this verse is that in the original Greek, is says, "And [it happened] they all wept sore, and fell on Paul's neck, and kissed him." The words "it happened" is a translation of the Greek word *ginomai,* which describes *something that arose unexpectedly; something not anticipated; something that took them off-guard.* The use of this word lets us know that when Paul and these leaders came together, they did not expect to become so deeply emotional.

Much to their surprise, the Scripture says, "they all wept sore..." (Acts 20:37). The phrase "wept sore" in Greek is *klauthmos,* which describes *bitter weeping; emotional weeping.* In their overwhelmed state, verse 37 says they "...fell on Paul's neck, and kissed him." The word "fell" is the Greek word *epipipto,* which means *to collapse upon.* And the word "kissed" in Greek is *kataphileo,* which literally means *to kiss down; to kiss fervently; to kiss profusely*; or *to cover with kisses*. This word indicates that the Ephesian leaders covered Paul with kisses — up one side and down the other.

With bitter weeping, they poured out their hearts and expressed their love and appreciation for him — knowing they would never see him again. Verse 38 confirms this, saying, "Sorrowing most of all for the words which he spake, that they should see his face no more…." The word "sorrowing" is a translation of the Greek word *odunao*, which is from the word *odune*, and it depicts *intense emotional pain* or *anguish*; *a great personal anguish expressed by great mourning*.

Their hearts were breaking because Paul said "…they should see his face no more…" (Acts 20:38). The word "see" is from the Greek word *theoreo*, which means *to gaze at*; *to look upon*; or *to discern*. It is the root for the word "theater." And the word "face" is the Greek word *prosopon*, which describes *the face* or *the countenance*. It means *to look at a person in the eyes*.

Imagine what the sight of Paul's face meant to these Christian leaders. They had focused on his countenance for three years as he stood in front of them teaching the Word of God. His was the face that led them out of bondage and into freedom in Christ. His was the face that disciple them daily. This would be the last time they would see him face-to-face and receive life-giving encouragement from his lips. Indeed, it was a deeply intimate and emotional exchange.

The Elders from Ephesus Accompanied Paul to the Ship

The Bible goes on to say, "…they accompanied him unto the ship" (Acts 20:38). The word "accompanied" is the Greek word *propempo*, which means *to accompany, conduct, escort*, or *to help one on his way*. Still deeply emotional that it would be the last time they would see Paul, all the leaders stayed with him right up to the moment he got into the ship to sail away. This was all part of the process of disconnecting and saying goodbye.

Acts 21:1 adds a little more detail about Paul's drawn-out departure. It says, "And it came to pass, that after we were gotten from them, and had launched…." The word "launched" in Greek is the word *anago*, and it means *to finally set out to sea*. More important is the phrase "after we were gotten from them." This is the Greek word *apospao*, which is a compound of the words *apo* and *spao*. The word *apo* means *away*, and the word *spao* means *to pull*. When the words are compounded, the new word *apospao* means *pulling away from*. It carries the idea of *withdrawing from*; *wrenching away from*; or *tearing away from*. The use of this word indicates a very difficult and emotional departure.

Again, these elders and leaders from Ephesus were people to whom Paul had given his life, and to know that they would never see him again was heart-wrenching. He literally had to tear himself away from them in order to board the ship and launch out into the new territory where God was taking him. This is the bittersweet picture of transition that often accompanies moving from where you are to the new place God wants you to be.

What does God have waiting for you? He said, "For I know the plans I have for you, says the Lord. They are plans for good and not for evil, to give you a future and a hope" (Jeremiah 29:11 *TLB*). Friend, there are new jobs, new dreams, and new opportunities ahead for you, but in order to experience them, you have to be willing to leave where you are and launch out in faith. Even though you won't know all that awaits you, you have God's promise that He will never leave you or forsake you. His amazing Holy Spirit will empower you and guide you every step of the way. Are you ready? It's time to launch out into new territory!

STUDY QUESTIONS

Study to shew thyself approved unto God, a workman that needeth not to be ashamed, rightly dividing the word of truth.
— 2 Timothy 2:15

1. When Paul met with the leaders of Ephesus for the last time, he positioned himself on his knees to pray with them. When was the last time you got down on your knees and poured your heart out to God? What were you praying about? Did you promise Him anything in exchange for answering your prayers?
2. Prayer is a powerful privilege and a vital practice for staying connected in relationship with God. According to Hebrews 10:19-22, what gives you the right to come before the throne of God in prayer? (Also consider Hebrews 9:11-14.) As per Ephesians 3:12 and Hebrews 4:16, how does God want you to approach Him in prayer?
3. Launching out into new territory can often produce thoughts and feelings of fear. But God doesn't want you to be afraid. He promises to

always be with you and take care of you. Take time to reflect on these promises He penned to you. How do they push back fear and encourage you to step out in faith?

- Hebrews 13:5,6; Genesis 28:15; Matthew 28:20
- Isaiah 54:10; Romans 8:31-39; John 10:27-30
- Joshua 1:5; Isaiah 43:1-5

PRACTICAL APPLICATION

But be ye doers of the word, and not hearers only,
deceiving your own selves.
—James 1:22

1. Rick shared how he and his family experienced two very difficult departures: when they left their family in the United States and moved to the former Soviet Union and when they moved from the city of Riga to Moscow. In what ways can you personally identify with the Renner's story?

2. Clearly, Paul's final moments with the leaders of the church of Ephesus were deeply emotional. Can you think of a time when you experienced a bittersweet departure like this? A moment when you became deeply emotional and it took you off guard? To whom were you saying goodbye? In what ways did God strengthen you to go on?

www.ingramcontent.com/pod-product-compliance
Lightning Source LLC
Chambersburg PA
CBHW051048030426
42339CB00006B/251